CW00742541

Help *Bereavement*

Christopher Herbert

COLLINS

All royalties from this book
will be paid to the
Basingstoke District Hospital Scanner Appeal.

Collins Liturgical Publications
8 Grafton Street, London W1X 3LA

Distributed in Ireland by
Educational Company of Ireland
21 Talbot Street, Dublin 1

Collins Liturgical Australia
PO Box 316, Blackburn, Victoria 3130

Collins Liturgical New Zealand
PO Box 1, Auckland

ISBN 0 00 599971 5
ISBN 0 00 599143 9 (pack of 10)
© 1987 Christopher Herbert
First published 1988

Typographical design Colin Reed
Cover illustration Malcolm Harvey Young
Typeset by K.G. Farren, Mill Street, Scarborough
Made and printed in Great Britain
by Bell & Bain Ltd, Glasgow

CONTENTS

INTRODUCTION

There is one absolute certainty in life, and that is, we shall all die. A fact of such universal importance can only be avoided for so long. Maybe the prospect of a death in your family or of one of your friends has prompted you to read this. Perhaps someone you know and love has already died and you find yourself having to cope with all the arrangements. Whatever your circumstances, I hope you will find here some practical help, some comfort in your sorrow, and maybe a renewal in your faith. When death comes it tests, like nothing else, everything that you believe. It challenges the way you live. It questions your values, but, as a result, it has the potential within it of new life. Even in the darkest hour of your grief you can be sure that the light will come. For the Christian that light is the knowledge that God will always be with you, no matter what depths you are in, and it is the light too of our Easter faith — that beyond the grave, through the boundless creativity of God, we shall, in Christ, be made new.

St Paul expressed it like this: 'I am convinced that there is nothing in death or life, in the realm of spirits or superhuman powers, in the world as it is or the world as it shall be, in the forces of the universe, in heights or depths, nothing in all creation that can separate us from the love of God in Christ Jesus our Lord' Romans 8.38-39.

Those words are as apt now as they were when written two thousand years ago. They are words of enormous and profound hope because they are, for the Christian believer, the words of truth.

Christopher Herbert

WHEN A DEATH OCCURS

There's no doubt that when a death occurs it comes as a great shock. You may be left wondering what you ought to do and where you ought to turn for advice. In the section which follows practical suggestions are made to help you cope with the first few hours and days. In order to make the information more easily accessible the chapter has been split up into sub-headings according to where the death has taken place e.g. at home, in hospital or abroad. You may want to skip those paragraphs which do not apply to your situation.

EXPECTED DEATH AT HOME

Contacting the doctor

If the death occurs at home the first person you should contact is the deceased's doctor. The doctor will come to you as soon as possible and, if the death has been expected, will issue a medical certificate concerning the cause of death. He or she will either give you that certificate immediately (it will be in a sealed envelope addressed to the registrar), or ask you to collect it later from the surgery, and you will also be given a notice telling you how to register the death with the registrar. The doctor will, at the same time, be able to tell you which registrar's office you need to attend.

Contacting the registrar

Once you have received the certificate your next duty is to go to the registrar to register the death. You will find the registrar's address and telephone number in the 'phone book under 'Registrar'. Alternatively, your Funeral Director will have all the details you need concerning the registrar's address, hours of opening etc. If by any chance you still cannot contact the registrar you could also ask your Citizens Advice Bureau, hospital, Post Office or the police for the information.

Visiting the registrar

It's worth finding out the times of attendance at the registrar's before you go to save yourself a wasted journey.

You will need to *take* with you
- the medical certificate of the cause of death
- the dead person's N.H.S. card (in the U.K.)
- any war pension book of the dead person.

You will also need to be able to *tell* the Registrar
- the date and place of death
- the address of the deceased
- full names and surname (if the dead person was a woman then also her maiden name)
- the deceased's date of birth and place of birth
- details of the deceased's occupation
- whether the dead person was receiving a pension or allowance from public funds
- if the dead person was married, the date of birth of the surviving widow or widower.

You will find the registrar very helpful and understanding in all this, and although it may take a little while to go through the formalities, it is important that they are done correctly.

Once the formalities are completed you will be *given*
- a certificate for disposal
- a certificate of registration of the death.

When you have that certificate of disposal you can then go to your Funeral Director and make arrangements for the funeral to take place. You may also want to contact your local vicar, minister or priest.

A summary of what you have to do may be helpful:
1 Call the deceased's doctor.
2 Receive from the doctor a medical certificate of the cause of death.
3 Go to see, or 'phone, your Funeral Director and, if you wish, your local vicar or minister.
4 Contact the registrar and arrange to go to the registrar's office.
5 Receive from the registrar a certificate of registration and a certificate of disposal.

You can see from the summary how much there is to be done — and when you feel in a state of shock you may not feel like coping on your own. If you have a near relative or close friend, call them as soon as you've called the doctor so that they can help you. You will also find that if you call your vicar or minister he or she will not only be able to help you practically but will also assure you of his or her prayers and the support and prayers of the Church too.

AN UNEXPECTED DEATH AT HOME

Contacting the doctor and the police

If the death at home is unexpected then you must contact the deceased's doctor immediately. You ought also to contact the police if the death was violent, accidental or if there are any suspicious circumstances. If the police are called do not touch or remove anything in the room.

The doctor may need to report the death to a coroner (a doctor or lawyer responsible for investigating certain deaths)
  - if the dead person was not attended by a doctor during his or her last illness or within 14 days of death
  - if the cause of death is uncertain
  - if the death was sudden, violent or caused by an accident
  - if death was caused by an industrial disease.

There are also other reasons for reporting the death to a coroner – so be guided by the advice and professional expertise of your doctor and the police in this.

The Coroner

The coroner has an office (the address can be obtained from the Citizens Advice Bureau, the police or the Funeral Director) which will give you the information and advice you need to know. You will be most unlikely to speak to the coroner himself but his officer (often a policeman or a retired policeman) will deal with the matter on his behalf. The coroner's officer will act as a liaison between the family and the coroner, helping to keep the family notified of procedures.

A postmortem

The coroner may arrange for a postmortem examination to take place in which he will try to establish the cause of death. If the death was due to natural causes he will issue a form for the registrar (the Pink Form), and he may either give this form to you direct to give to the registrar or send it to the registrar himself.

If the death was violent or caused by an accident or industrial disease, or if after the postmortem the cause of death is still uncertain, he will hold an inquest.

An inquest

An inquest is a public event, sometimes with a jury, in which the court tries to establish the cause and circumstances of the death.

It is important to note that when an inquest is held it may be some days, weeks or even months after the death. When this happens the family cannot register the death until the inquest has taken place, but to allow families to deal with outstanding business — insurance claims for example — the coroner may issue a letter to the family which enables them to do so.

You, as a relative, can attend the inquest and, with the permission of the coroner, ask questions of the witnesses. You can also be represented at the inquest by a lawyer — it may be important to have a lawyer representing you if the death was caused by a road accident or an accident at work which could lead to a claim for compensation.

Other duties of the Coroner

The coroner will also:
1 Give an order for burial or a certificate for cremation to the nearest relative.
2 Send a certificate-after-inquest to the registrar, stating the cause of death.
3 Give, on request, a letter confirming the fact of death.
4 Give permission (if necessary) for the body to be moved out of the country.
5 Pay for the removal of the body from the place of death to the mortuary for a postmortem examination.

A summary of this section may help:
1 Call the deceased's doctor immediately.
2 In the case of violent, accidental or suspicious circumstances call the police.
3 The doctor may report the case to a coroner.
4 If he does there will probably be a postmortem.
5 If the death was due to natural causes the coroner will issue a form for the registrar.
6 If the death was violent, caused by an accident, industrial disease, or if after the postmortem the cause of death is still uncertain, he will hold an inquest.

Again, as with all professional people concerned with death, the coroner and the coroner's staff will be helpful and understanding, though, as you will appreciate, they have a job to do and have to follow the procedures of that job with care.

A DEATH IN HOSPITAL

When a death occurs in hospital the nursing staff (usually the sister-in-charge) will give you advice about what you have to do. Normally you will be asked to go to the Hospital Administration department where you will be able to collect the death certificate and any of the personal belongings of the deceased. The death certificate will be given to you if the cause of death is clear. But the doctor may ask your permission, if you are the nearest relative, to carry out a postmortem if the cause of death is uncertain, or if death was sudden, violent, or caused by an accident or industrial disease. There will also have to be a postmortem if the death occurred while the patient was undergoing an operation or was under the effect of an anaesthetic. If a postmortem is necessary, the doctor will report the death to the coroner − and the procedures followed will be as in the paragraph above concerning the coroner.

It may also be the case that the doctor will ask the family's permission to carry out a private postmortem or a clinical postmortem. Whilst the doctor knows the cause of death he or she may feel that such a postmortem would confirm his or her findings or would aid medical research.

It is worth noting that if the death occurs in an evening or over a weekend or Public Holiday you may not be able to see anyone at the hospital until normal working hours are resumed. This may mean a delay in making arrangements for the funeral. However you can usually contact a Funeral Director (most offer a 24-hour service) to discuss the situation and ask for advice.

WHEN A DEATH OCCURS ABROAD

Registering the death

Obviously local custom will dictate what you should do but you will need to register the death according to the local regulations in the country and get a death certificate. You must also register the death with the British Consul so that a record of the death is kept in England. You will be able to get a copy of this later from the General Registrar Office at St Catherine's House, 10 Kingsway, London WC2 6JP.

Where to have the burial or cremation

You will have to decide whether or not to have local burial or cremation, or whether to bring the body back to the U.K. once you have received either the death certificate or an authorisation to remove the body from the country of death from the coroner or equivalent.

If you arrange a funeral in England or Wales you will need either an authenticated translation of a foreign death certificate or a death certificate issued in Scotland or Northern Ireland as well as a certificate of no liability to register from the Registrar in England or Wales in whose sub-district it is intended to bury or cremate the body.

In fact all of this will normally be dealt with by the Funeral Directors and they will notify the coroner in whose area the funeral is to take place. He may decide upon a further postmortem, even if an examination has taken place abroad, and this can cause further delays. Your Funeral Director may be able to obtain a form of authorisation from the Home Office (Queen Anne's Gate, London) for cremation only. Although this sounds complicated you will find a number of people able and willing to help you. For instance there are a number of repatriation specialists — companies used by the major airlines and tour operators — who are involved from the start and they will give every assistance to the bereaved relatives.

All of these practical details may seem a bit official and daunting. They are not meant to be, and the people wearing the official hats will try to make the situation as bearable for you as possible. If you have any questions about any of these procedures ask either your Funeral Director or your vicar or minister for help.

When a body is to be donated to medical research

Some people make it very clear, before they die, that they wish their body to be used for medical research or for some of their organs to be donated. In this case, if the death is normal i.e. at home and expected, or in hospital and expected, then the nearest relative will have to act with some speed to make sure these wishes can be carried out. For instance, kidneys must be removed by the proper medical authorities within half an hour and eyes within six hours. Where the death has to be reported to the coroner his consent will be necessary before either organs or body are donated.

When a body is being donated to medical research, normally the deceased's doctor will, at your request, contact H.M. Inspector of Anatomy, alternatively the Funeral Director may do so. It is however possible, though unusual, for the nearest relative to contact the Inspector (H.M. Inspector of Anatomy, Eileen House, Newington Causeway, London SE1, tel. 01 703 6380).

It must be said that although the deceased person may have sincerely requested that the body be used for research it may not always be possible to comply with the request — but again either the doctor or the Funeral Director will be able to advise you in these circumstances. Where a body is used for teaching or research it must be buried or cremated within two years — the relevant medical school will tell you about this when you liaise with them about accepting the body.

ARRANGING THE FUNERAL

FINDING A FUNERAL DIRECTOR

Once you have registered the death you will need to turn your attention to the funeral and contact a Funeral Director. You may already know a Funeral Director whom you trust, or you may be able to ask friends and relatives for their advice. If you have no one to ask you could contact your local vicar or minister for help in choosing, although he or she will try to be as careful as possible in not suggesting one firm rather than another. You will find that Funeral Directors are highly experienced, sympathetic and understanding and will give you help in your decisions. To ensure the very best advice you would be well advised to choose a Funeral Director who is a member of the National Association of Funeral Directors. They have a code of practice adhered to by their members, including strict observance of confidentiality and the rendering of good service.

When you have seen the Funeral Director it is usual for you (or, if you prefer, the Funeral Director) to make contact with your vicar, minister or priest. He or she will arrange to meet you at a convenient time to offer practical advice, counsel and support, and to arrange the funeral service.

ARRANGING THE PLACE FOR THE SERVICE

Depending on your personal beliefs, or the requests of the deceased, you are entitled to choose from a variety of services. There are a range of possibilities open to you and your vicar or minister will be able to discuss them with you. In general you can have:
1 A service in church or chapel followed by cremation and interment of ashes or burial in a cemetery.
2 A service in a cemetery chapel (where available) followed by burial.
3 A service in a crematorium chapel followed at some later date by the burial of the ashes.
What you decide to do will be determined largely by your tradition and your beliefs. If you are a church-goer it is likely that you will want the main part of the funeral service to be held in your place of worship, not least

because there you will be surrounded by your friends and by the signs of the Christian faith.

THE SERVICE ITSELF

Choosing a service

Again, depending on local custom, you will want to decide the kind of service with your vicar or minister. If you are an Anglican you have a large choice of services available — from traditional Book of Common Prayer to the varieties offered by the *Alternative Service Book 1980*. If you are Free Church there are also a range of options — including the Funeral Service prepared by the Joint Liturgical Group, an ecumenical body. If you are Roman Catholic there is a specific Funeral Rite available for use at a crematorium or cemetery when there is no Mass. It is impossible to be specific in a book like this but in general you will also need to consider:
  – your choice of hymns and psalms
  – your choice of Biblical reading
  – whether or not you wish for an address (sermon) to be given.

Devising your own service

Some people like to construct a funeral service which is entirely of their own making; but if they want their minister to take part this ought to be done only with his or her full co-operation and support. The funeral services of the Churches have been well thought out and developed over the centuries and as a result have a depth and strength which 'one-off' services rarely achieve.

Having the order of service printed

You might like to consider having the service printed (your Funeral Director and minister can help you with this), including the hymns, readings and the music you decide on. It will then be a reminder to you in the future of the service. You may feel that you will never forget which hymns you chose, for instance, but memory can and does play tricks, and a printed order of service to which you can refer may bring some solace.

BURIAL OR CREMATION?

Usually in their wills people state whether they wish to be cremated or buried. If they have not done so then you may want to check with friends, neighbours or relatives to see if they have any memory of what the deceased might have wanted. Where there is no mention in a will, and nothing in writing anywhere else, the decision is left to the executor or nearest relative. It should be noted that if the deceased has left written instructions that cremation is not desired then those wishes must be adhered to.

Cremation

The majority of people these days prefer cremation. They see it as both dignified and sensible. The ashes can be disposed of according to the expressed wishes of the deceased (within reason), but normally they are buried in a churchyard, a cemetery or a garden of remembrance. In some cemeteries and gardens headstones or memorial plaques are allowed — but this varies from area to area. Some people prefer to scatter the ashes in a favourite spot chosen by the dead person. If this spot is a private garden, it's worth considering whether, if the house and garden are later sold, the relatives will feel uneasy about leaving the ashes behind. To avoid this it may be wiser to choose a public and designated burial ground. If no instructions have been left then the disposal is arranged by either an executor or the nearest relative.

Burial

If the dead person has indicated that they wanted to be buried you will need to discover if they have already paid for a grave space. If they have they should have one of two documents: either a 'faculty' — if the grave is in a churchyard, or a 'deed of grant' if the grave is in a cemetery administered by a local authority or a private company. If neither of those documents can be found then you will have to purchase a grave space. In the case of a churchyard the vicar or rector has the right to decide where the grave will be, and you will also be told of the regulations concerning headstones etc. A grave in a public cemetery may also be subject to regulations concerning headstones and memorials etc.

Whilst burial is less popular than it used to be, some people prefer the strong sense of 'place' which burial can give to the mourners. It is somewhere to visit, to look after; a place for remembering.

PAYING FOR THE FUNERAL

When you first visit the Funeral Director you should ask for an estimate of what the funeral will cost. Clearly that estimate will vary according to what you want to do, and you will be told what the estimate covers and the items it omits, as well as the time by which the final bill has to be paid.

Funerals can be very expensive and you should ensure that you know where the money for those costs will come from. The D.H.S.S. will advise you about death grants, or if you are eligible for help from the Social Fund. Your local Citizens Advice Bureau will also be more than pleased to assist you with any questions you may have, and to help you apply for grants if you are entitled to them.

FLOWERS OR CHARITY?

There was a time when everyone going to a funeral arranged for a wreath of flowers to be sent. On the whole, the pattern now is for the close family to give flowers and for the other mourners to give donations to the charity of the family's choice. An announcement about this is often included in the 'Births, Marriages and Deaths' column of newspapers, or you can have cards printed to send to the mourners beforehand.

When flowers are requested, it is often suggested after the service that they be given to a local hospital or church. The Funeral Director will be able to advise you about the suitability of this. Some wreaths, for instance, cannot easily be dismantled for use in a vase, and some hospitals find themselves overwhelmed with flowers.

Where gifts of money are made instead of flowers, it makes life simpler if a 'Treasurer' can be appointed to keep a record of the donations on behalf of the family and to handle the distribution of the money to the charity afterwards.

WHEN THE VICAR CALLS

When the vicar, minister or priest calls to see you before the funeral, he or she is there to help in whatever way possible and also to guide you both about the service and about any questions you have. It's often helpful if you ask what actually happens at the service — so that you can picture in advance what will take place.

Don't hesitate either to ask those questions of belief or faith which trouble you. You may not want to do this before the funeral, but your vicar or minister would be very willing to come to see you in the weeks that follow to assist you in your grief and in facing the world again. If you don't wish to discuss these things with your minister, there may be others to whom you can turn e.g. trained lay-people either in the Church or in secular organisations who will be equally willing to listen and to help, if necessary (addresses for some of these organisations are at the back of this book).

ON THE DAY OF THE FUNERAL

The service

The Funeral Director will make sure that all the arrangements go very smoothly. He will escort you to the place of the service (if you so wish) and will be on hand to deal with any last-minute alterations to your plans.

At the church or chapel your vicar, minister or priest will be there to greet you and to lead you and the mourners through the service. You may not feel like taking a vocal part at all, on the other hand you may feel that the singing of the hymns or the saying of the prayers are exactly what you want and need to do. Whatever happens, the clergy are there to assist you in the act of worship, and they will be praying for you before, during and after the service. To be held in the fellowship of the prayers of the Church is a source of deep spiritual strength.

The party

It is wise and good to have a gathering after the funeral where food and drink can be shared — partly for memories to be talked over, and partly because this is a way of expressing solidarity one with another. Traditions concerning funeral parties vary from one area of the country to another — from massive sit-down feasts to the simplicity of a cup of tea. Only you can decide what is appropriate for your situation.

THE STAGES OF GRIEF

A very large number of books and articles have been written about grief during the past few years. Most of them refer, quite rightly, to the stages of grief. But it needs to be pointed out that whilst there are stages in grieving not everyone follows the same pattern. Many of the stages overlap, and many of the stages are 'revisited' by the person who has been bereaved — often when they least expect it. In this section we shall be looking at these stages, but it needs to be re-emphasised that to call something a 'stage' suggests a definite beginning and end, whereas in reality it's all much more confused with one stage merging with another.

SHOCK

When someone dies the people left behind often go into a state of shock and numbness. When describing this later they say things like, 'My legs just turned to jelly', or, 'I suddenly went very cold inside', or, 'It was like a blow'. You'll recognise those comments as soon as you've read them. Sometimes the shock is not instantaneous, but is delayed for hours, days or weeks. When it does happen, do not be surprised by it and try not to pretend that it's not happening. It is perfectly normal to be in a state of shock and not something of which you need feel ashamed. Neighbours and friends can be a great help simply by being with you and making sure that you keep warm and are as comfortable as possible. To know that even though the whole world seems to have fallen apart there are family and friends around is in itself a help.

NUMBNESS

'I felt it wasn't happening to me. I was inside looking out watching everything going on like in a play' is how some people have described the numbness and detachment they felt. C.S. Lewis in his book *A Grief Observed*, written after his wife died, said this:
'No one ever told me that grief felt so like fear. I am not afraid, but the

17

sensation is like being afraid. The same fluttering in the stomach, the same restlessness, the yawning. I keep on swallowing.

At other times it feels like being mildly drunk or concussed. There is a sort of invisible blanket between the world and me. I find it hard to take in what anyone says.'

This numbness can actually be helpful. It doesn't feel like it, but it seems to be our way of filtering the awful news so that only those parts of it that we can deal with are allowed through — for the moment. The trouble is that it's often when feeling most numb that major decisions have to be made. Again, if family and friends are around they can help you to make those decisions. But it's important that the decisions are made with you. If family and friends busy themselves, thinking that they are doing the right thing by leaving you alone, the chances are it will not be done as you would wish. Much patience and understanding are required on all sides.

DISBELIEF

In the beginning you may have a strange sense of disbelief. 'I just can't believe it. I just can't believe it', and others say things like, 'I expect him to come through the door at any minute' or, 'I found myself laying two places for supper'. The sense of disbelief, very, very strong at first gradually gives way to occasional but often very vivid experiences which are often described as 'silly'. (They aren't silly at all.) 'I waited by the phone for her to call' or, 'I kept thinking I might see him in the street'. There's no denying that loss is acute. It hurts terribly and often when people find themselves doing 'silly' things they wonder if they're going out of their mind. Again, that too is a very common and understandable reaction, and it is perfectly normal.

Those first three stages of shock, numbness and disbelief weave themselves together and the person going through them wonders what on earth is happening. From a Christian point of view the experience is one that was shared by Jesus himself, at the loss of his friend Lazarus, and by Mary and the disciples at the loss of Jesus. God, as we know him in Jesus Christ, goes with the sufferer through the sufferings. God doesn't avoid it nor stand aloof from it. God is there, yoked to you, helping you to carry the burden and taking much of its weight upon his shoulders.

'THE LONG SEARCH'

'I used to go to the town where we had first lived', he said, 'in the hope that I would see her. I kept looking. Everywhere. Looking and looking.'

The sense of loss is often expressed in a kind of aching yearning search for the person who has died. That search may be a physical one, like the widower quoted above, or it may be psychological. And it's often accompanied by bouts of anger, frustration, tiredness, and, perhaps, by feelings of guilt. ('If only . . .'.) The anger may be directed at God ('Meanwhile', as C.S. Lewis wrote: 'Where is God? . . . Why is he so present a commander in our time of prosperity and so very absent a help in time of trouble?'), or at other people — the doctor, the hospital, the family, or at oneself. Sometimes the anger is expressed by comparing the virtues of the person who has died with the vices of those left alive. 'He was so good. Why should he die when people who mug old ladies live?' And from time to time the anger is directed at the clergy — who are seen as somehow colluding with God in letting someone die.

The frustration that accompanies all this may be connected with having to do things which have never before had to be tackled — everything from turning the water stop-cock off to dealing with cheques and bills. ('He always did it, and now I feel so hopeless.') Others talk of their memories not being so good as before: 'I keep forgetting things. I put the key down and don't remember where I put it. I even forget which day of the week it is.'

'And as for tiredness', say the bereaved, 'I'm exhausted all day and can't wait to get to bed and as soon as I get there I lay awake all night.' For others there is an opposite reaction — not tiredness but frantic activity: a restless desire to get everything done at once and to be thoroughly organised. And then there are those feelings of guilt: 'If only . . .', 'If only I'd been there', 'If only we'd spent more time together', or that feeling of guilt which comes from being the survivor. (This was expressed vividly in my hearing by a young widow who only minutes after her husband's death said simply 'Beam me up, Scottie'.)

All those feelings then — of anger and frustration and tiredness and guilt — go slopping around. We seem to have little control over them. We try, but the smallest memory can bring them flooding back. Again, for the Christian there are ways of acknowledging all those feelings — by talking about them to a counsellor, minister or wise friend; and there is too the assurance that no matter how appalling we believe our feelings to be — the truth is in his wisdom God has created us as we are. God knows our feelings, he knows our weaknesses, he knows those moments when we seem to be careering into an abyss. It's in those moments that God, perhaps to our surprise, seems more present than ever before – not taking away the hurt, not pretending it hasn't happened, but simply being there with us. 'And underneath are the everlasting arms.' And the God of Jesus Christ is one who assures us not only of understanding but also of forgiveness – our guilt can be transformed by forgiveness into the seeds of new life.

'FLOODS OF TEARS'

In her book, *Through Grief*, Elizabeth Collick writes:

'Johnnie was the first disturbed child with whom I was professionally involved. He was nine years old and motherless. One of his symptoms was that he stole and then gave or threw away what he had stolen. One day he rushed into the room of his favourite therapist with a new football which he dumped on the table and then, crying uncontrollably, he buried his face in the therapist's lap. "Now I wonder," she said, almost speculatively, "just why you wanted that football." After a long tense pause Johnnie jumped up. "I've got a big, big hole right *here*," he said, and thumped himself hard just below his ribs as he stamped round the room in angry frustration.

Johnnie's "big, big hole" was an emptiness at least as big as the football; it could never be filled – not, that is, by anything but the love that he had lost.

I recognised Johnnie's pain some thirty years later in the hollow ache of my own heart. I have heard its echoes often since as the bereaved have tried to express their sense of desolation, though never quite so dramatically as when a group of widowed people were comforting an elderly man who had lost his wife only two or three weeks earlier. With a sad shake of his head he said, "It's like a big empty hole right here" and hugged his arms to his chest.'

That big empty hole sometimes seems just that. Empty. Dry. ('I just can't cry.') And at other times it seems to fill up like a dam with flood water. From time to time the waters pour over the top or the dam bursts. 'I keep crying all the time. I just can't help it' or, 'I'm fine until someone says something and then I've had it' or, 'It's alright when people are matter-of-fact, when they're sympathetic I break down.' The tears are there to be released – not in any hysterical fashion but because they help to ease the tension and express the devastating sense of loss which afflicts the bereaved. For those near by the temptation may be to say something like, 'Buck up' or, 'Don't cry'. Those are not necessarily helpful things to say or to hear.

For the Christian, the example of Jesus himself weeping should give permission, if such is needed, for the bereaved to realise that weeping is good and acceptable, and if you recall the story of St Peter at the Passion he too went outside and 'wept bitterly'. To weep is as God-given an ability as to smile.

REMEMBERING

When the first frantic days or weeks are past the bereaved often want to talk, to remember their beloved. They may repeat themselves time and time again and tell the same story, but as the days go by they will want to expand their repertoire and remember not only very recent events but also events in the distant past. They will want to recall good days as well as bad ones. The tendency for the listener is to be impatient, particularly with the frequent repetitions, but to be able to help the bereaved to reminisce in a way that is safe and healing is a great gift.

ACCEPTANCE AND LOOKING FORWARD

The final stage is not so much a stage as a new way of looking at life. It's as though you have been in a long dark tunnel and you come out of it into a new country. You can't go back to the old, but there is a new land waiting. The discovery of this new land is partial and sometimes a little confused. It doesn't happen in an instant but comes little by little, and it comes as the reality of the death is accepted deep down inside our personalities. That takes time, a degree of courage, and surprisingly, a sense of humour. But come it does and as the acceptance deepens so does the awareness that life goes on and there are new things waiting to be done. For the Christian there is the awareness of still being led by God. That's not to deny that the road has been very rough and jagged, but God continues to lead, to uphold you and to cherish you and will remain with you in your new state.

'Lo I am with you always', said our Lord: 'even to the end of time.'

MEANWHILE, WHERE IS GOD?

C.S. Lewis in *A Grief Observed* expressed the anguish of the bereaved like this:

'Meanwhile, where is God? This is one of the most disquieting symptoms. When you are happy, so happy that you have no sense of needing him, so happy that you are tempted to feel his claims upon you as an interruption, if you remember yourself and turn to him with gratitude and praise, you will be – or so it feels – welcomed with open arms. But go to him when your need is desperate, when all other help is vain, and what do you find? A door slammed in your face, and a sound of bolting and double bolting on the inside. After that, silence. You may as well turn away.'

Which is, you have to admit, strong stuff, especially from a Christian writer of C.S. Lewis' brilliance. But he does unwaveringly point to a disquieting experience – that appalling and abysmal sense of God's absence when you feel you need him most. It is echoed, with even greater agony, in Christ's own cry of dereliction from the Cross: 'My God. My God. Why hast Thou forsaken me?'

It is so difficult to suggest an answer in the face of that kind of desolation which doesn't just seem trite or smug or plain evasive. To be fair to Lewis, he does attempt an answer later in his book. He suggests that the very noise and clamour of his call to God might have prevented him hearing: 'You are like the drowning man who can't be helped because he clutches and grabs.' But he goes on from that to explore the idea that we have to let go of the images of God we have so that the reality of God can take hold of us: 'My idea of God is not a divine idea. It has to be shattered time after time. He shatters it himself. Could we not almost say that this shattering is one of the marks of his presence?' In other words, what appears to be the absence of God is not that at all, it is the absence of our empty ideas about God, we have to let go of those ideas so that God himself can confront us and cherish us in his love and truth. Not easy. But necessary if we are to have a real relationship with him. Let it be said again: if you feel that absence, the absence is real. But it might be God's way of saying 'Look in another direction, from another angle and find me there.'

Which is perhaps a not very comforting way to think of the presence of God. In a crisis you might expect him to be so much with you. He is, and yet he seems to want us, especially in these moments, to trust him even in the depths. If you like, to trust his absence so that his true presence may be revealed to us. Another way of putting it is to say that when you are at rock bottom you discover the rock.

What kind of God then is it in whom we believe? We believe in God as Creator — and around us we see a universe in a constant state of change, the old gives way to the new, winter gives way to spring, death seems to be the root-source of life. In that sense the death of someone we love is part of a universal pattern — and we believe that that pattern is part of the Being of God, part of his expression of love in the universe. A mystery we cannot comprehend, but a mystery into which we enter.

But we believe too in God not as a Creator who is a kind of cosmic engineer creating and yet remaining outside his creation; all the evidence we have from the Bible, from the earliest times, is of a God who astonishingly wants to be, and is, in relationship with his creatures. In the beautiful myth of Genesis he is pictured as 'walking in the Garden in the cool of the day'; in speaking to Moses in the Burning Bush he discloses his identity, 'I am', and throughout the Old Testament God yearns for and works with and cherishes his chosen people. He is by no means an absent God. Quite the reverse. A God who loves, a God who cares for the peoples he has brought into being. Then, in the life of Jesus, we see God incarnate. God makes himself much clearer, so to speak. He reveals himself as a servant, as one who suffers with and for mankind, as one who loves the poor, the maimed, the blind and who brings healing to body, mind and soul. The God whom we see in Jesus is a God of absolute and unending compassion, who loves the world so much that he offers himself as the redeemer. He is a God who knows what it is to be human from the inside, who knows pain and grief and desolation, who knows anguish and heartbreak and pain.

For the Christian, God is especially with us when we are at our most broken and desolate. John Austin Baker, Bishop of Salisbury put it like this:

'I rest on God who will assuredly not allow me to find the meaning of life in his love and forgiveness, to be wholly dependent on him for the gift of myself and then destroy that meaning, revoke that gift. He who holds me in existence now can and will hold me in it still, through and beyond the dissolution of my mortal frame. For this is the essence of love, to affirm the right of the beloved to exist. And what God affirms, nothing and no one can contradict.'

We see then in God the Creator a God who holds us in being. We see in Jesus Christ's life on earth, the love of that God − full of grace and truth. But we don't just stop there in our beliefs. We go on to look not only at Jesus' human life this side of death, we look too at the way he brought to us a faith built upon the Easter event. Death was defeated by Jesus at the resurrection: he was brought through death by God and in his new and risen life revealed the gift of resurrection for mankind. We do not model our beliefs simply upon Jesus the good man, but upon Jesus the Saviour. It is at this point that inevitably words slip and slide. It's not surprising. An event as stupendous as the resurrection is going to strain language to the uttermost. Which is why we need to turn to others to see how they have tried to express it. Here is St Paul in his letter to the early church in Rome:

'In view of all this, what can we say? If God is for us, who can be against us? Certainly not God, who did not even keep back his own Son, but offered him for us all! He gave us his Son − will he not also freely give us all things? Who will accuse God's chosen people? God himself declares them not guilty! Who, then, will condemn them? Not Christ Jesus, who died, or rather, who was raised to life and is at the right-hand side of God, pleading with him for us! Who, then, can separate us from the love of Christ? Can trouble do it, or hardship or persecution or hunger or poverty or danger or death? As the scripture says,

'For your sake we are in danger of
    death at all times;
we are treated like sheep that are
    going to be slaughtered.'

No, in all these things we have complete victory through him who loved us! For I am certain that nothing can separate us from his love: neither death nor life, neither angels nor other heavenly rulers or powers, neither the present nor the future, neither the world above nor the world below − there is nothing in all creation that will ever be able to separate us from the love of God which is ours through Christ Jesus our Lord.'

It is in those magnificent words from scripture that we glimpse the truth of our faith: God in Jesus Christ breaks the bonds of death and gives us the assurance of life everlasting. A promise that even through the darkest of darknesses the light of resurrection will shine. A promise that death is not the end but a new and glorious beginning.

SOME THOUGHTS AND PRAYERS

In bereavement we often look around for help from those who have been there before us. We want to know what they felt like, how they coped. The readings and prayers which follow may be of some help in this process. They need to be read slowly and thoughtfully. It is quite likely that one of them will be particularly apt and you will return to it again and again for solace.

READINGS

Death is nothing at all . . . I have only slipped away into the next room. I am I and you are you. Whatever we were to each other that we are still. Call me by my old familiar name, speak to me in the easy way which you always used. Put no difference in your tone; wear no forced air of solemnity or sorrow. Laugh as we always laughed at the little jokes we enjoyed together. Play, smile, think of me, pray for me. Let my name be ever the household word that it always was. Let it be spoken without effort, without the ghost of a shadow on it. Life means all that it ever meant. It is the same as it ever was: there is absolutely unbroken continuity. Why should I be out of mind because I am out of sight? I am waiting for you for an interval, somewhere very near, just around the corner. All is well.

Henry Scott Holland

Dear A,
    . . . I meant to buy a wreath. But somehow couldn't face going into the shop and saying: 'No, I think tulips would be nicer.' So, I never went. Also there was the card. I didn't know what to write. 'Sympathy . . .? Deepest . . .?' Deepest what? I couldn't leave it blank and I couldn't write: THIS CAN'T BE THE END.

That's what came over me all the time: THIS CAN'T BE THE END.

It wasn't thinking back to remembered times, or because I felt — I'll keep him alive in my heart. It was more. It was much more. More than anything I knew about life up to the moment he died. It was the way his death brought a new dimension, and a hope. I knew there was more. I became sure. And somehow I couldn't send a wreath.

So I'm sitting down trying to apologise for this seeming neglect, darling. Because for you, God knows what it means — an emptiness? Is there any conviction through the crucifixion? Is there a prelude being played for the mysterious comprehension: THIS CAN'T BE THE END?

But surely I was wrong, a wreath is not finality but rather flowers promising a glory, a symbol of eternity. They, too, die to speak of this awareness of otherness. They witness the dispelling of gloom when one hears the thunderous awakening words:
THE RISING FROM THE TOMB.
And in this silent thrill, there is the excitement of an adventure ahead, suddenly, nothing to dread.

I regret not sending a wreath.

Anne Shells

Trying to be cheerful — because I missed her badly — I went wearing a red hat to the memorial service of Daisy Knight Bruce. It was a mistake. I knew how wretched the last few weeks of her life had been, and there were only one or two others in that packed church who also knew this, so I reckoned we were gathered to give thanks for her life and rejoice. However, I felt conspicuous and managed to squash the hat into my handbag — or did I? After all these years I honestly don't remember whether I sat it out or bowed to convention. Churchgoers are always being faced with this problem, if not with hats any more, at least with a great many more important issues.

But then it is amazing how some church people behave in church; it's as though they leave their familiar selves outside the door and become most unnatural. Of course at most funerals the mourners have little confidence in the readings and prayers and are in any case in a state of distress, but the following conversation cannot be so unusual:

Many years and funerals since Daisy Knight Bruce's, I remember brave Mrs Grey. They had not long retired when Mr Grey died.
'So, Mr Grey has passed away.'
'Isn't it sad about Mr Grey.'
'Poor Mrs Grey . . .'

'Just after he was getting a little better.'

Oh, how they went on.

But Mrs Grey said:

'I'm glad for him, dear, you see he would never have gone on with his garden. He was a good man. I know he is better off where he is.'

That's what Mrs Grey said.

But the others went on,

'It's dreadful about Mr Grey, isn't it?'

They were STILL saying it after the funeral, after singing the hymns and hearing the statement:

Jesus said: THOUGH HE DIE, YET SHALL HE LIVE,
AND WHOEVER LIVES AND BELIEVES IN ME
SHALL NEVER DIE.

So when someone said to me: 'Oh, I do think it is so awfully sad about Mr Grey', I could bear it no longer. I said, 'But you go to church every Sunday, don't you believe? Whatever do you think church is all about?' And got the reply:

'Well, no one has ever come back, have they?'

'NO ONE HAS EVER COME BACK? JESUS CAME BACK!'

To which I got the answer:

'He was God.'

'But he was MAN!'

At that point it seemed better to mention the jumble sale, and let the Holy Spirit take over.

Anne Shells

I may be able to speak the languages of men and even of angels, but if I have no love, my speech is no more than a noisy gong or a clanging bell. I may have the gift of inspired preaching; I may have all knowledge and understand all secrets; I may have all the faith needed to move mountains — but if I have no love, I am nothing. I may give away everything I have, and even give up my body to be burnt — but if I have no love, this does me no good.

Love is patient and kind; it is not jealous or conceited or proud; love is not ill-mannered or selfish or irritable; love does not keep a record of wrongs; love is not happy with evil, but is happy with the truth. Love never gives up; and its faith, hope, and patience never fail.

Love is eternal. There are inspired messages, but they are temporary; there are gifts of speaking in strange tongues, but they will cease; there is knowledge, but it will pass. For our gifts of knowledge and of inspired messages are only partial; but when what is perfect comes, then what is partial will disappear.

When I was a child, my speech, feelings, and thinking were all those of a child; now that I am a man, I have no more use for childish ways. What we see now is like a dim image in a mirror; then we shall see face to face. What I know now is only partial; then it will be complete — as complete as God's knowledge of me.

Meanwhile these three remain: faith, hope, and love; and the greatest of these is love.

St Paul: 1 Corinthians 13

Easter Wings

Lord, who created man in wealth and store,
though foolishly he lost the same,
decaying more and more,
till hc became
most poor,

with thee
Oh let me rise,
as larks, harmoniously,
and sing this day the victory:
then shall that fall further the flight in me.

My tender age in sorrow did begin,
and still with sickness and shame
thou didst so punish sin
that I became
most thin.

With thee
let me combine,
and feel this day thy victory:
for if I graft my wing on thine,
affliction shall advance the flight in me.

George Herbert

The Moment of Ecstasy

This life is a period of training, a time of preparation, during which we learn the art of loving God and our neighbour, the heart of the Gospel message, sometimes succeeding, sometimes failing.

Death is the way which leads us to the vision of God, the moment when we shall see him as he really is, and find our total fulfilment in love's final choice.

The ultimate union with that which is most lovable, union with God, is the moment of ecstasy, the unending 'now' of complete happiness. That vision will draw from us the response of surprise, wonder and joy which will be forever our prayer of praise. We are made for that.

Basil Hume

(*Christian and Hopeful have come through the river of death.*)

Now upon the bank of the river, on the other side, they saw the shining men again, who there waited for them. Wherefore being come out of the river, they saluted them, saying, We are ministering spirits, sent forth to minister for those that shall be heirs of salvation. Thus they went along towards the gate.

Now you must note, that the City stood upon a mighty hill; but the pilgrims went up that hill with ease, because they had these two men to lead them up by the arms; also they had left their mortal garments behind them in the river; for though they went in with them, they came out without them. They therefore went up here with much agility and speed, though the foundation upon which the City was framed was higher than the clouds; they therefore went up through the regions of the air, sweetly talking as they went, being comforted because they had safely got over the river, and had such glorious companions to attend them.

The talk that they had with the shining ones was about the glory of the place: who told them that the beauty and glory of it was inexpressible. There, said they, is the Mount Sion, the heavenly Jerusalem, the innumerable company of angels, and the spirits of just men made perfect. You are going now, said they, to the paradise of God, wherein you shall see the tree of life, and eat of the never-fading fruits thereof: and when you come there you shall have white robes given you, and your walk and talk shall be every day with the King, even all the days of eternity. There you shall not see again such things as you saw when you were in the lower region upon the earth: to wit, sorrow, sickness, affliction and death; for the former things are passed away. The men then asked, What must we do in the holy place? To whom it was answered, You must there receive the comfort of all your toil, and have joy for all your sorrow; you must reap what you have sown, even the fruit of all your prayers, and tears, and sufferings for the King by the way. In that place you must wear crowns of gold, and enjoy the perpetual sight and visions of the Holy One; for there you shall see him as he is. There also you shall serve him continually.

John Bunyan, *The Pilgrim's Progress*

It is all grace. It is not even that there is a door which Christ has unbolted, and we, standing outside it, have to stretch out our hand, lift the latch, and walk through. We are already inside. When our Saviour became man and undid the sin of Adam, he did not command the cherubim with the flaming sword to return to heaven so that we could re-enter Eden. He picked up the walls of Eden and carried them to the farthest edge of Ocean, and there set them up so that they now girdle the whole world. All we are asked to do is to open our eyes and recognise where we are. Once we have done that, then we shall look down at ourselves and our filthy bodies and our tattered clothes, and we shall say, 'I am not fit to be here, in Paradise'; and we shall ask for baptism to wash us clean, and for the white robe of chrism to clothe us in the righteousness of the Lord. But not in order that we may be saved — simply because this is fitting for those who have been saved.

John Austin Baker

I rest on God, who will assuredly not allow me to find the meaning of life in his love and forgiveness, to be wholly dependent upon him for the gift of myself, and then destroy that meaning, revoke that gift. He who holds me in existence now, can and will hold me in it still, through and beyond the dissolution of my mortal frame. For this is the essence of love, to affirm the right of the beloved to exist. And what God affirms, nothing and no one can contradict.

John Austin Baker

Death, be not proud, though some have called thee
  Mighty and dreadful; for thou art not so.
  For those whom thou think'st thou dost overthrow
  Die not, poor Death, nor yet can'st thou kill me.
  From rest and sleep, which but thy pictures be,
  Much pleasure, then from thee much more must flow;
  And soonest our best men with thee do go —
  Rest of their bones, and soul's delivery.

  Thou art slave to Fate, chance, kings and desperate men,
  And dost with poison, war, and sickness dwell;
  And poppy or charms can make us sleep as well
  And better then thy stroke; why swellst thou then?

One short sleep past, we wake eternally
And death shall be no more; Death, thou shalt die.

John Donne

In the Midst of Life

Death and I are only nodding acquaintances
We have not been formally introduced
But many times I have noticed
The final encounter
Here in this hospice,
I can truly say
That death has been met with dignity.
Who can divine the thoughts
Of a man in close confrontation?
I can only remember
One particular passing
When a man,
With sustained smile,
Pointed out what was for him
Evidently a great light.
Who knows what final revelations
Are received in the last hours?
Lord, grant me a star in the East
As well as a smouldering sunset.

Sidney G. Reeman

Via Dolorosa

Do not make the mistake
  of imagining that you
  may go singing
  on the Via Dolorosa
  neither may you
  bear right or left
  the way is confined
  with little room
  for manoeuvre

You will know exhaustion
  kneeling often
  trodden and rough
  and scarred by many feet
  this way is our way
  and may not be shunned
  turned from
  or avoided
  best to go quietly
  with a dogged courage
  knowing that
  one thing is certain:
  There is an end

And when you arrive
  you will find
  that the hill is crowned
  with a living tree
  stretching out
  great branches
  to give you shelter
  and manna there
  and spring water

Margaret Torrie

If I should go before the rest of you,
Break not a flower nor inscribe a stone.
Nor when I'm gone speak in a Sunday voice,
But be the usual selves that I have known.
Weep if you must,
Parting is hell,
But life goes on,
So sing as well.

Joyce Grenfell

Psalm 23

The Lord is my shepherd: therefore can I lack nothing.

He shall feed me in a green pasture: and lead me forth beside the waters of comfort.

He shall convert my soul: and bring me forth in the paths of righteousness, for his name's sake.

Yea, though I walk through the valley of the shadow of death, I will fear no evil: for thou art with me; thy rod and thy staff comfort me.

Thou shalt prepare a table before me against them that trouble me: thou hast anointed my head with oil, and my cup shall be full.

But thy loving-kindness and mercy shall follow me all the days of my life: and I will dwell in the house of the Lord for ever.

Glory be to the Father, and to the Son: and to the Holy Ghost;

As it was in the beginning, is now, and ever shall be: world without end. Amen.

If the Great Father Creator is as great as death,
surely as creator of the universe, of darkness and light,
he must be at least equal to his creation;
and in so being,
as an artist is greater than his canvas,
so is he greater than death.

Giles Harcourt

PRAYERS

It is a common experience that when we most need to pray, especially in times of grief, the words simply won't come. A bereaved man, Jim Parfitt, in the video film *Beneath the Surface* (Collins) told how even the Lord's Prayer seemed to be impossible to say after the death of his wife, but that going to church and saying it with others made sense. The strength of prayer is that even when you yourself can not pray the Church will pray for you and with you.

Into that house they shall enter
and in that house they shall dwell
where there shall be
  no cloud nor sun
  no darkness nor dazzling
but one equal light;
  no noise or silence
but one equal music;
  no fears or hopes
but one equal possession;
  no foes nor friends
but one equal eternity.

Keep us, Lord,
so awake in the duties of our callings
that we may thus sleep in thy peace
and wake in thy glory.

John Donne

O my God, I have no idea where I am going. I do not see the road ahead of me . . . Nor do I really know myself, and the fact that I think I am following your will does not mean that I am actually doing so. But I desire to do your will, and I know the very desire pleases you. Therefore, I will trust you always though I may seem to be lost. I will not fear, for you are always with me, O my dear God.

Thomas Merton

Eternal Light, shine into our hearts,
Eternal Goodness, deliver us from evil,
Eternal Power, be our support,
Eternal Wisdom, scatter the darkness of our ignorance,
Eternal Pity, have mercy upon us;
    that with all our heart and mind and soul and strength
    we may seek thy face and be brought
    by thine infinite mercy to the holy presence;
    through Jesus Christ our Lord.

Alcuin

Lord, all these years we were so close to one another, we did everything together, we seemed to know what each was feeling, without the need of words, and now she is gone. Every memory hurts . . . sometimes there comes the feeling that she is near, just out of sight. Sometimes I feel your reproach that to be so submerged in grief is not to notice that she is as eager to keep in touch with me, as I with her. O dear Lord, I pray out of a sore heart that it may be so, daring to believe that it can be so.

George Appleton

Grant, O Lord, to all those who are bearing pain, thy spirit of healing, thy spirit of life, thy spirit of peace and hope, of courage and endurance. Cast out from them the spirit of anxiety and fear; grant them perfect confidence and trust in thee, that in thy light they may see light; through Jesus Christ our Lord.

Anon

Almighty God, Father of all mankind,
in your Son you took upon yourself
the world's sorrow.
We offer you our own sorrow and sadness
knowing that you can help us to bear our grief
through the infinite understanding and love
of Jesus Christ our Lord.

Christopher Herbert

35

Help in your Bereavement

We seem to give them back to you, O God, who gave them to us . . . Yet as you did not lose them in giving, so we do not lose them by their return. O lover of souls, you do not give as the world gives. What you give you do not take away; for what is yours is ours also if we are yours. And life is eternal and love is immortal; and death is only a horizon; and a horizon is nothing save the limit of our sight. Lift us up, strong son of God, that we may see further; cleanse our eyes that we may see more clearly; draw us closer to yourself that we may know ourselves to be nearer to our loved ones who are with you. And while you prepare a place for them, prepare us also for that happy place, that where you are we may be also for evermore. Amen

Bishop Charles Henry Brent

Go forth upon thy journey from this world, O Christian soul,
    in the peace of him in whom thou hast believed,
    in the name of God the Father, who created thee,
    in the name of Jesus Christ, who suffered for thee,
    in the name of the Holy Spirit, who strengthened thee.
May angels and archangels, and all the armies of the heavenly host,
    come to meet thee,
may all the saints of God welcome thee,
may thy portion this day be in gladness and peace, thy dwelling in
    Paradise,
Go forth upon thy journey, O Christian Soul.

Prayer for the dying, from the Roman Ritual

Christ is the morning star who
when the darkness of this world is past
brings to his saints
the promise of the light of life
and opens everlasting day.

The Venerable Bede

Lord, support us all the day long in this troublous life, until the shades lengthen, the evening comes, the busy world is hushed, the fever of life is over, and our work is done. Then, Lord, in your mercy grant us safe lodging, a holy rest, and peace, at the last, through Jesus Christ our Lord. Amen

John Henry Newman

Father in heaven, you gave your Son Jesus Christ to suffering and to death on the cross, and raised him to life in glory. Grant us a patient faith in time of darkness, and strengthen our hearts with the knowledge of your love; through Jesus Christ our Lord. Amen

Alternative Service Book 1980 (A.S.B. 1980)

Father of all, by whose mercy and grace your saints remain in everlasting light and peace: we remember with thanksgiving those whom we love but see no longer; and we pray that in them your perfect will may be fulfilled; through Jesus Christ our Lord. Amen

A.S.B. 1980

Almighty God, Father of all mercies and giver of all comfort: deal graciously, we pray, with those who mourn, that casting all their care on you, they may know the consolation of your love; through Jesus Christ our Lord. Amen

A.S.B. 1980

O Father of all, we pray to thee for those whom we love, but see no longer. Grant them thy peace; let light perpetual shine upon them; and in thy loving wisdom and almighty power work in them the good purpose of thy perfect will; through Jesus Christ our Lord. Amen

Book of Common Prayer (1928)

O heavenly Father, who in thy Son Jesus Christ, hast given us a true faith, and a sure hope: Help us, we pray thee, to live as those who believe and trust in the Communion of Saints, the forgiveness of sins, and the resurrection to life everlasting, and strengthen this faith and hope in us all the days of our life: through the love of thy Son, Jesus Christ our Saviour. Amen

Book of Common Prayer (1928)

For this reason I fall on my knees before the Father, from whom every family in heaven and on earth receives its true name. I ask God from the wealth of his glory to give you power through his Spirit to be strong in your inner selves, and I pray that Christ will make his home in your hearts through faith. I pray that you may have your roots and foundation in love, so that you, together with all God's people, may have the power to understand how broad and long, how high and deep, is Christ's love. Yes, may you come to know his love — although it can never be fully known — and so be completely filled with the very nature of God.

To him who by means of his power working in us is able to do so much more than we can ever ask for, or even think of: to God be the glory in the Church and in Christ Jesus for all time, for ever and ever! Amen

Ephesians 3.14-21

SELECTED BIBLIOGRAPHY

Ainsworth-Smith and Speck, Peter, *Letting Go*, SPCK
Autton, Norman, *Readings in Sickness*, SPCK
Bowman, Harold, *Living through Grief*, Lion
Collick, Elizabeth, *Through Grief*, Darton, Longman and Todd
Lewis, C.S., *A Grief Observed*, Faber and Faber
Saunders, Cicely, *Beyond all Pain*, SPCK
Whitaker, Agnes, *All in the End is Harvest*, Darton, Longman and Todd

D.H.S.S. leaflet D49/Aug 79, *What to do after a death*. Available from D.H.S.S. Offices and from the D.H.S.S. Leaflets Unit, PO Box 21, Stanmore, Middlesex, HA7 1AY